CW01512636

Original title:

Morning Reflections

Author: Olivia Orav

ISBN HARDBACK: 978-1-80560-277-4

ISBN PAPERBACK: 978-1-80560-742-7

Echoes of a New Day

Whispers of light begin to play,

A gentle breeze starts to sway.

Birds sing songs of hope and cheer,

Awakening dreams, drawing near.

Shadows flee from the dawn's embrace,

New beginnings fill the space.

Rising Hues in the Sky

Crimson and gold paint the air,

Morning's brush strokes, soft and rare.

Each color dances, a vibrant show,

As nature wakes from night's deep glow.

Clouds drift slowly, whispers in flight,

Transforming the canvas of twilight.

A Canvas of Soft Dawn

Tender hues spread across the land,

Awakening dreams with a gentle hand.

Mountains stand tall in the morning light,

Guarding the secrets of the night.

Fields of dewdrops glisten and gleam,

A beautiful start to every dream.

The Quiet of Early Hours

Silence cradles the world in peace,

Time slows down, worries cease.

Soft footsteps tread on paths of dew,

While the heart knows what is true.

A whisper of hope in every breath,

The calm before life's lively depth.

The Dance of New Beginnings

In the morning's gentle breeze,
Fresh bids of hope take flight.
Leaves whisper secrets of dawn,
As shadows fade from sight.

Softly blooms the vibrant flower,
Breaking through the coldest ground.
Each petal tells a story sweet,
Of dreams yet to be found.

The sun spills gold on quiet streams,
Awakening the silent earth.
A symphony of light and charm,
Sings of life and rebirth.

Hands raise high towards the skies,
Embracing all that's new.
Every heartbeat, every sigh,
A promise to renew.

In the dance of the wide expanse,
Hope waltzes with the day.
With each step, a chance to grow,
And find the joy in play.

Poetry Slumbering in Light

In the stillness of the night,
Words drift soft and low.
Beneath the vast, starry quilt,
Dreams begin to flow.

Whispers wrapped in twilight's glow,
Stir the sleeping soul.
Each line a gentle caress,
Making shadows whole.

The moon spills silver on the page,
With verses yet to find.
Lines curled like autumn leaves,
Awake in quiet mind.

Time pauses, breaths unite,
In the dance of silent art.
Each stanza stirs the quiet heart,
Crafting worlds apart.

As dawn approaches, softly bright,
The poem takes its flight.
In every inked embrace,
Resides the dawn's sweet light.

Chasing Shadows Before Noon

In the quiet morn, we tread so light,
Shadows dance beneath the warming light.
Whispers call from the trees so wise,
We chase the dreams that softly rise.

The sun climbs high, the shadows play,
Fleeting moments drift away.
Each footfall echoes tales of old,
In this realm where hearts unfold.

Leaves rustle gently in the breeze,
Nature's sigh brings subtle ease.
We run through glades, with laughter pure,
A fleeting joy that feels so sure.

Time slips by like sand in glass,
But we'll remember as we pass.
Chasing shadows, our spirits soar,
In this dance, we find our core.

As noon approaches, shadows fade,
Yet in our hearts, they've softly laid.
Memories linger, sweet and true,
In every chase, I find you too.

Nature's Awakening Chorus

Dewdrops cling to morning grass,
Sunrise paints the sky to pass.
Birds start singing vibrant tunes,
Nature wakes to brightened moons.

Trees stretch high, their branches sway,
Colors burst in bright array.
Flowers bloom, a gentle sigh,
In this moment, life is nigh.

Streams murmur with a joyful sound,
In harmony, the world is found.
Each creature joins the festal glee,
Nature's chorus, wild and free.

Clouds drift by, soft shadows cast,
A symphony, the die is cast.
The earth rejoices, life anew,
In every heartbeat, we renew.

As day unfolds, our spirits lift,
Nature's song, a precious gift.
Together in this vibrant space,
Awakening, we find our place.

When the World Exhales

In the twilight, silence hums,
Deep breaths linger, time succumbs.
Stars peep out in the azure night,
The world exhales, releasing light.

Whispers travel on the breeze,
In the stillness, hearts find ease.
Gentle waves lap at the shore,
Each moment beckons us for more.

Moonlight silver on the land,
Nature's calm, a steady hand.
Thoughts drift like clouds across the sky,
In this peace, we learn to fly.

Closing eyes, we breathe it in,
Letting go of where we've been.
Surrendered to the night's embrace,
In the darkness, we find grace.

When the world sighs, we align,
In the quiet, souls intertwine.
Each heartbeat echoes through the vast,
In this harmony, we are cast.

Serene Beginnings

Morning light breaks, soft and kind,
Whispers of hope float on the wind.
A new day dawns, fresh and bright,
Serene beginnings take their flight.

The world awakens, gentle and slow,
Nature's palette begins to flow.
Colors dance in a radiant scheme,
Blankets of wonder, stitched with dreams.

Birds take wing, a joyous greet,
In harmony, they find their beat.
Each note swells, fills the air,
With every sound, we find our care.

As soft winds breeze through the trees,
Sowing seeds of sweet release.
In this moment, hearts entwine,
With every breath, a chance to shine.

Serenity wraps the earth so tight,
Encouraging souls to find their light.
With open arms, we seize the day,
In these new beginnings, we choose to stay.

Chasing the Night's Remnants

In twilight's embrace, shadows play,
Whispers of dreams in fading gray.
Stars gleam softly, their secrets unfold,
Chasing the night's remnants, brave and bold.

Moonlight dances on the silent sea,
Echoes of laughter, wild and free.
The cool breeze carries a sweet refrain,
Chasing the night, we forget our pain.

In the hush, a lingering sigh,
Moments like fireflies flit by.
Each heartbeat quickens, the spell is cast,
Chasing the remnants, holding fast.

Through darkened paths where shadows creep,
Promises whispered, secrets to keep.
With every step, we feel the might,
Chasing the night's remnants, into the light.

Flickers of Gold

In the dawn's glow, the world awakes,
Colors emerge, the stillness breaks.
Flickers of gold on leaves that sway,
Nature sings softly, welcoming day.

Clouds part gently, the sun shines bright,
Casting shadows, embracing light.
In gardens blooming, life unfolds,
Moments like treasures, flickers of gold.

Bees hum merrily, skies widen clear,
Whispers of spring beckon us near.
With every breath, new stories told,
Capturing the magic, flickers of gold.

A warmth envelops, the heartbeats race,
In every corner, a sacred space.
As time flows softly, memories hold,
Cherished forever, flickers of gold.

Serenade of the Lark

In the early light, a song takes flight,
A lark on the wing, pure delight.
Notes fill the air, rise to the blue,
Serenade of the lark, ever true.

Melodies woven with whispers of breeze,
Nature applauds with rustling leaves.
Each chord a promise, every trill bold,
In harmony's embrace, stories unfold.

With valleys below and peaks all around,
The lark's sweet refrain is nature's own sound.
Beneath the vast heavens, so uncontrolled,
The serenade brings warmth as hearts behold.

Awakening dreams, igniting the soul,
In the hush of morn, we feel the whole.
As time softly flows, each moment's gold,
In the serenade, love untold.

Lifting the Night's Shroud

As soft twilight settles, the stars ignite,
The moon, a beacon, guides through the night.
With each gentle breeze, shadows awake,
Lifting the night's shroud, dreams we make.

Crickets sing low in the stillness profound,
Echoing secrets the darkness surrounds.
A moment of silence, emotions unfold,
Lifting the shroud, our stories told.

In the glow of lanterns, heartbeats align,
Glimmers of hope in the stars that shine.
With every breath, whispers of old,
Lifting the night's shroud, the brave and bold.

Through the velvet sky, in shadows we drift,
Carried by dreams, a celestial gift.
As dawn gently breaks, our spirits uphold,
Lifting the night's shroud, hearts of gold.

Waking Dreams and Sighs

In the quiet morn I rise,
With dreams that dance like fireflies.
Soft whispers from the night,
Fade away with the dawn's light.

Memories linger in the air,
A sigh escapes without a care.
Awakening the heart so deep,
As gentle waves of daylight sweep.

Eyes open to the tender scene,
Where shadows blend with vibrant green.
Each breath a promise to embrace,
The magic found in this vast space.

Amidst the stillness, hope ignites,
As day replaces starry nights.
I gather dreams from slumber's hold,
And greet the world, both new and bold.

Nature's Symphony at Daybreak

The sun peeks through the leaves so bright,
Awakening the world to light.
Birdsong fills the crisp, cool air,
A symphony of wild flair.

Whispers of the morning breeze,
Rustle through the ancient trees.
Gentle streams begin to flow,
As nature puts on her grand show.

Colors burst in vibrant hues,
Painting skies with morning blues.
Each note played in perfect tune,
Beneath the watchful eye of noon.

Fields of flowers sway and dance,
In this playful, fleeting chance.
Nature's heart, a rhythmic beat,
Inviting all to take a seat.

The Brush of Time on a New Day

With dawn, the canvas starts anew,
A palette rich with morning dew.
Time's brush paints the world so bright,
In colors soft, a pure delight.

Shadows stretch, then fade away,
As dreams from night begin to sway.
The golden light begins to rise,
Transforming all before our eyes.

Moments linger, slipping fast,
Yet memories hold strong and vast.
Each hour ticks a gentle rhyme,
In the soft embrace of time.

Fleeting hours we hold so dear,
Collecting echoes year by year.
The brush of life, a tender hand,
Sketching dreams across the land.

Raindrops Still Cherished

Softly falling from the skies,
Raindrops dance, like whispered sighs.
Each drop a story, pure and sweet,
A fleeting kiss on earth's heartbeat.

Puddles form, reflections shine,
Nature's tears, both yours and mine.
They quench the thirst of every bloom,
In earth's embrace, dispelling gloom.

Clouds gather, a symphony loud,
Chasing joy from the sun's shroud.
Yet in their midst, a calm prevails,
As the beauty of the rain unveils.

Raindrops glide on petals soft,
In their embrace, we drift aloft.
Each drop a reminder of the grace,
Found in each storm, in every space.

Dewdrops on Silent Windows

Dewdrops cling like precious gems,
Glistening softly in the dawn,
Silent whispers of the night,
Nature's canvas waits for light.

Each droplet tells a story,
Of midnight's soft embrace,
Morning's breath begins to stir,
Awakening the world's grace.

The window frames a gentle view,
Where time stands still, afresh,
Moments captured in the glass,
Beauty held in quiet mesh.

As sunlight warms the earth anew,
The dewdrops start to fade,
Their transient dance, a silent truth,
In this delicate charade.

Awakening Whispers

In the hush before the dawn,
Awakening whispers softly speak,
The world stirs from its slumber,
Secrets that the shadows keep.

Glimmers of hope in the air,
With each gentle rustle and sigh,
The heart listens for the call,
Of dreams that are meant to fly.

Buds begin their brave ascent,
A tapestry of blooms unfolds,
Nature's brush with vibrant shades,
Each color a story told.

The sun peeks in with a smile,
A dance begins, the day awakes,
With every note of morning's choir,
Life rejoices in the breaks.

The Sun's Gentle Embrace

Softly shines the sun's warm glow,
Kissing the earth with tender grace,
Its embrace a golden robe,
Warming every cherished place.

Casting shadows long and soft,
Every corner feels alive,
Together with the gentle breeze,
In harmony, we thrive.

The sky blushes a deeper hue,
As clouds drift lazily by,
A moment wraps the world in peace,
Beneath the vast, embracing sky.

Sundrenched paths we care to roam,
Each step a dance with fate,
The sun's light guides our journey forth,
In its arms, we contemplate.

First Light's Serenade

With a whisper, the day unfolds,
First light paints the sky in gold,
A serenade of peace and hope,
In nature's arms, our hearts behold.

Love sings through the rustling leaves,
Awakening dreams long kept asleep,
As dawn's brush strokes the horizon,
Over the valleys wide and deep.

Mountains wear a misty veil,
While rivers glisten, soft and bright,
Every note of morning calls,
The world alive, bathed in light.

In this melody of the morn,
Each heartbeat dances to the tune,
First light's serenade invites us,
To cherish life's sweet afternoon.

Quiet Contemplations Amidst the Birds

In the morn, the whispers sing,
Fluttering wings, a gentle ring.
Thoughts like clouds, drift above,
Wrapped in peace, a thread of love.

Bright sunlight bathes the scene,
Nature's grace, a vivid green.
Songs of life, both near and far,
Echo soft, as dreams ajar.

Each note dances in the air,
Moments cherished, light and rare.
Lost in wonder, hearts laid bare,
Finding calm, free from despair.

In every chirp, a story flows,
Nature's art, in droplets shows.
Contemplations weave and swirl,
In the stillness, minds unfurl.

Lifting the Curtain of Night

Stars retreat, a fading glow,
As dawn breaks with a vibrant show.
The moon whispers its soft goodbye,
Awakening dreams to the sky.

A breath of light, the world ignites,
Shadows fade, lost in the heights.
The horizon, a canvas new,
Painted in shades of morning dew.

Hope arises with the sun's crest,
A promise of what lies, the best.
Every moment, a chance to rise,
To embrace the day with open eyes.

The chorus of life begins to hum,
A symphony of all that's come.
In this dance of dusk to dawn,
We find our way, forever drawn.

New Beginnings in Flickering Glimmers

In twilight's glow, where dreams ignite,
New paths emerge, in soft twilight.
Each pause, a promise to unfold,
A tale of courage, brave and bold.

Glimmers spark in hearts awake,
Casting fears like gentle flake.
With every dawn, a chance reborn,
From shadows past, the light is sworn.

Whispers of hope, like silver threads,
Weaving futures in soft spreads.
In every breath, a chance we chase,
New beginnings find their place.

Life's river flows, a constant stream,
Guiding us to the edge of dream.
In every flicker, we discover,
The strength within, like no other.

The Breath of Possibility

In silence, the world holds its breath,
Awaiting moments, life and depth.
A heartbeat stirs within the still,
The dawn of dreams, the void to fill.

Possibilities dance in the unknown,
Seeds of hope, gently sown.
Each choice whispers a tale untold,
The future glimmers, brave and bold.

In every step, the path unfolds,
A journey rich with dreams and gold.
With every sigh, we rise and fall,
A tapestry woven, for one and all.

Embracing chances, taking flight,
In the darkness, we seek the light.
Fear fades softly, as courage grows,
In the breath of life, possibility flows.

Caffeine and Quiet

Steam rises from a cup,
Morning whispers softly,
Thoughts awaken with the light,
A quiet space, a gentle start.

The world outside is rushing,
But here I find my peace,
With each sip, a moment,
A sip to fuel my mind.

Pages turn with harmony,
Ideas dance in shadows,
In this hush, I ponder,
Dreams brew like strong coffee.

Time drips like honey slow,
Each moment treasured keen,
A small retreat from chaos,
In caffeine's warm embrace.

With every bitter sip,
I find a notion clear,
Caffeine and a whisper,
In quietude, I thrive.

Reflections of a New Canvas

The brush tip dances lightly,
Colors splash like laughter,
Each stroke tells a story,
A canvas waits with breath.

Sunlight spills through windows,
Inspiring hues arise,
A masterpiece emerging,
In silence, dreams take flight.

Lines and shapes encounter,
In playful, vibrant cheer,
Each flaw becomes a feature,
In art, we find our truth.

The palette mixes softly,
Bright greens and sunset gold,
Every shade a heartbeat,
A life reborn anew.

With every twist of color,
A world begins to bloom,
The canvas holds my secrets,
A reflection of my soul.

Nostalgic Hues

In faded shades of memory,
I wander through the past,
A whisper of the laughter,
Joy echoing through time.

Golden afternoons linger,
With shadows softly drawn,
Pictures in sepia tones,
Each frame, a gentle touch.

The scent of rain on pavement,
Reminds me of sweet youth,
Chasing clouds with wild hearts,
In a world free and bright.

Those nostalgic hues embrace me,
Like a well-loved song,
Every note brings comfort,
And time becomes a dream.

In quiet reflection,
I cherish all that's gone,
Forever in my colors,
Nostalgia paints my heart.

Petals Dropping with Grace

Delicate petals flutter,
In the softest of breezes,
Each one a whispered secret,
Falling down like soft rain.

Beneath the cherry blossom,
A carpet of pure dreams,
Every hue tells a story,
Of love in gentle spring.

The world slows for a moment,
As petals dance in air,
An elegant surrender,
To the rhythm of the day.

With every graceful landing,
Life's beauty finds its place,
Nature's fleeting reminder,
To embrace the present space.

In the silence that follows,
A whisper lingers near,
Petals dropping with such grace,
An artful end, sincere.

The Color of Tomorrow

In hues of red and gold, we dream,
A canvas bright, with endless gleam.
Hope paints the skies with every glance,
A promise waits, a second chance.

Beneath the clouds, the shadows play,
Whispers of light, they lead the way.
Emerald fields stretch far and wide,
In nature's grace, we find our stride.

With every dawn, a fresh start brings,
A symphony of life that sings.
The palette rich, with stories bold,
Each stroke tells tales yet to unfold.

We gather colors from the air,
In heart's embrace, a world laid bare.
Together hand in hand we stand,
In the light, we make our plans.

So let the future be our muse,
In vibrant shades, we cannot lose.
With every breath, we paint the scene,
The color of tomorrow, bright and clean.

Sunlit Pathways

Golden rays are breaking through,
Warming hearts and spirits too.
A journey starts with each new day,
Along these sunlit pathways, we stray.

Beneath the trees, shadows play,
As laughter dances down the way.
The world aglow, time stands still,
With every step, our dreams fulfill.

Flowers bloom, their colors bright,
Guiding us with pure delight.
The wind's soft touch, a gentle guide,
In nature's arms, we find our pride.

Each moment shared, a memory made,
In sunlight's grip, we will not fade.
Hand in hand, we walk with grace,
Together, we create our space.

So let us wander, hearts unbound,
In these bright pathways, joy is found.
The sun above, a constant light,
Guiding us safely through the night.

Resisting the Night

When shadows fall and dreams take flight,
We find the strength to resist the night.
Stars flicker bright, a guiding spark,
In the dark, we leave our mark.

With whispered hopes, we chase the gloom,
Finding light in every room.
Courage rises with the moon,
In stillness, we will find our tune.

Each heartbeat strong, beats back the dread,
With every step, our fears are shed.
Together we stand, side by side,
Choosing paths where love can guide.

Through every struggle, we will soar,
Embracing all that lies in store.
For darkness cannot claim our light,
We shine on through the endless night.

So hold my hand, and do not fear,
Together, we will persevere.
In the night's embrace, we ignite,
A flame of hope that burns so bright.

Embracing Tender Solitude

In quiet moments, gently we find,
The beauty of peace that calms the mind.
Embracing stillness, hearts can heal,
In tender solitude, we feel.

Whispered thoughts like softest sighs,
Dance through the air and softly rise.
A sanctuary within us grows,
In solitude, true wisdom flows.

Each breath a gift, a chance to pause,
To cherish silence without cause.
Moments gathered like pearls of light,
In solitude, we find our might.

Alone but whole, a truth we gain,
In gentle peace, we shed the pain.
To love ourselves, a sacred quest,
In solitude, we are truly blessed.

So here we stand, in quiet grace,
Embracing solitude's warm embrace.
In stillness, we discover the art,
Of nurturing the tender heart.

Whimsy in the Air

Dancing leaves on playful breeze,
Flutter by with such a tease.
Laughter echoes through the trees,
Joyful hearts that roam with ease.

Clouds take shapes in skies so blue,
Imagination's dancing crew.
Every moment feels anew,
Whimsy's touch in all we do.

Giggling streams flow with delight,
Sunshine sparkles, pure and bright.
Nature whispers, soft and light,
Inviting dreams to take their flight.

Butterflies in vibrant hues,
Painting paths with nature's views.
Chasing shadows, back and forth,
Whimsy weaves its magic worth.

Evenings glow with twinkling stars,
Stories shared from near and far.
Every wish a tiny spar,
Sprinkling joy like falling stars.

A New Day's Promise

Morning breaks with golden light,
Whispers soft, the world feels right.
Hope awakens with the day,
Chasing all the dreams away.

Birds sing sweetly from the trees,
Carrying a gentle breeze.
Nature's canvas, fresh and bright,
Painting dawn with hues of light.

Steps of morning, sweet and slow,
Cradled in a gentle glow.
Each heartbeat syncs with the sun,
A new journey has begun.

Clouds drift softly, dreams take flight,
Whispers of the day's delight.
Every moment filled with grace,
A new day's warm embrace.

With each breath, fresh hope we find,
Life unfolds, forever kind.
In the stillness, joy we borrow,
A new day's promise shapes tomorrow.

Unfolding Like Petals

Morning dew on petals gleam,
Nature dances, life's sweet dream.
Colors bloom in soft array,
Unfolding hope with each new day.

Gentle winds caress the flowers,
Whispers sweet in gentle hours.
Each petal shares a tale untold,
In every hue, a world unfolds.

Sunlight kisses every hue,
Painting dreams in shades so true.
Life's embrace in every bloom,
Unfolding joys that chase the gloom.

In the garden, hearts are free,
Nature's song, a symphony.
Each new blossom, a delight,
Unfolding worlds in purest light.

Every day a chance to grow,
In love's embrace, we gently flow.
Unfolding like the dawn's first ray,
In nature's arms, we find our way.

Wandering Thoughts

In my mind, the echoes roam,
Wandering far from place called home.
Thoughts like clouds drift through the air,
Searching for what isn't there.

Scattered dreams on gentle waves,
Nostalgia sings, the heart it saves.
Moments lost in fleeting time,
Yet each memory feels like rhyme.

Paths untraveled call me near,
Whispers soft, I stop to hear.
Curious hearts seek what they lack,
Wandering thoughts always track back.

In the silence, dreams ignite,
Bringing shadows into light.
Every wonder, every sigh,
Tethered dreams that long to fly.

Through the labyrinth of my mind,
Wandering thoughts, I seek to find.
In the maze, both bold and frail,
A journey woven, soft and pale.

Dawn's Whispering Canvas

The horizon blushes, soft and bright,
Whispers of daybreak chase the night.
Colors unfurl on a gentle breeze,
Nature awakens with tranquil ease.

Birds begin singing, a sweet serenade,
As shadows retreat, the light starts to fade.
Petals unfold in their delicate grace,
Embracing the warmth of the sun's warm embrace.

Golden rays dance on the dew-kissed grass,
Time feels suspended in this moment, alas.
Hope paints the sky in hues anew,
A canvas of dreams in soft morning blue.

Clouds drift lazily, like thoughts in our mind,
Each stroke a reminder of what we might find.
Awake in the stillness, with hearts open wide,
In dawn's gentle light, we find where we bide.

The world breathes softly, a lullaby sung,
In dawn's tender palette, our souls feel young.
Every heartbeat echoes, with potential to rise,
As dawn whispers secrets beneath waking skies.

Glimmers of Light in the Quiet

Silent moments cradle the night,
Soft glimmers emerge, pure and bright.
Stars twinkle gently, a celestial dance,
In the stillness, we find our chance.

Whispers of hope echo in the dark,
Flickering shadows ignite a spark.
Dreams take flight on the wings of the dawn,
Each glimmer a promise, a new day reborn.

Moonlight bathes the world in silver hue,
Illuminating paths where thoughts wander through.
In the cocoon of night, we gather our dreams,
As light drips softly from the cosmic beams.

Moments of magic, elusive yet near,
Entwining our hearts in the silence we hear.
Glimmers that beckon, a call from afar,
Inviting us closer, like a guiding star.

We tread lightly, wrapped in the peace,
Finding solace in shadows that never cease.
A tapestry woven with light's tender touch,
In the quiet, we linger, embracing so much.

Awakening Dreams

In the hush of twilight, dreams softly bloom,
Awakening whispers dispel all the gloom.
Cascading colors paint the night sky,
As wishes take flight on the moon's gentle sigh.

Every heartbeat pulses with fervent delight,
A symphony woven in the fabric of night.
Stars wink above in a playful embrace,
Guiding our thoughts to a magical place.

Awake in the moment, we dare to explore,
With eyes wide open, unearthing what's more.
Each dream a story, waiting to be told,
In the land of the night, where our hopes unfold.

The night wraps around us, a silken cocoon,
In the realm of enchantment, where dreams are in tune.
We gather our courage, we venture outside,
In the tapestry woven, we take our sweet ride.

As dawn approaches, we hold onto the thread,
Of dreams that awaken, guiding us ahead.
In the glow of the morning, new paths will gleam,
With the promise of life, we cherish our dream.

When the Sky Blushes

When the sky blushes in shades of pink,
The world holds its breath, pausing to think.
Clouds adorned in amber, a painter's hand,
Etching soft memories across the land.

The sun stretches slowly, yawning awake,
Awakening colors that twinkle and shake.
Night retreats gently, a whispered goodbye,
As dreams settle down with a sweet lullaby.

Rays spill like secrets, warming the ground,
In this moment of beauty, silence is found.
Birds herald the day with jubilant song,
In the blush of the sky, we all feel we belong.

The horizon embraces the light's tender embrace,
In the symphony played by the dawn's gentle pace.
Each heartbeat echoes with hope in the air,
When the sky blushes, we gather to share.

With every new dawn, a chance to renew,
To embrace the potential in all that we do.
So let us rise up, in the warmth of its glow,
For when the sky blushes, our spirits will grow.

The Horizon's Silver Lining

In twilight's gentle glow we wait,
The sky adorned with threads of fate.
A whisper soft, a promise clear,
Silver lining draws us near.

With every dawn, the shadows fade,
Across the seas, our hopes cascade.
A painted path, so rich and wide,
We chase the dreams that ever guide.

The colors blend, a sacred art,
As day begins to play its part.
With each new breath, we feel the sway,
The horizon beckons us to stay.

In silence deep, the stars align,
Reflections dance, so pure, divine.
Our hearts entwined in cosmic play,
Together, we embrace the day.

Within the glow of morning's light,
The world awakens, future bright.
With hands held tight, through time we soar,
Towards the dreams forevermore.

Fresh Pages in the Book of Day

The sun breaks through with golden rays,
Each moment starts a new embrace.
With every dawn, hope's light appears,
Fresh pages turn, we face our fears.

In vibrant hues, the morning sings,
A symphony of simple things.
With laughter shared and stories spun,
A brand new day has just begun.

The ink of night starts to dissolve,
As mysteries of day evolve.
With open hearts, we wander free,
In every step, our spirits flee.

The winds of change begin to blow,
With every line, our visions grow.
A tender heart and open mind,
In love's embrace, our dreams aligned.

We pen the tales of joy and strife,
In this great book, the art of life.
With every page, the past gives way,
To endless hope, a brighter day.

Radiant Hues of Happiness

In gardens bright, where flowers bloom,
Their colors chase away the gloom.
Each petal whispers secrets true,
In radiant hues, life's vibrant view.

The laughter shared beneath the trees,
Is carried gently by the breeze.
Like painted skies as daylight glows,
In every heart, pure joy bestows.

With every smile, a spark ignites,
A dance of warmth in heart's delights.
The world becomes a canvas bright,
As colors brush away the night.

In moments small, in simple grace,
We find the truth, the warm embrace.
In radiant hues, we learn to see,
The beauty that forever be.

With open arms, we greet the day,
In every heartbeat, love's ballet.
May happiness in colors blend,
A timeless joy that knows no end.

Beneath the Grasp of Sunbeams

The morning dew on blades of grass,
Reflects a light that's meant to last.
With sunbeams bright, we find our grace,
In nature's fold, a warm embrace.

The shadows melt as warmth descends,
In golden light, our spirit mends.
We run through fields, the air so sweet,
Each moment shared feels so complete.

In laughter loud, the world takes flight,
With sun-kissed dreams that feel so right.
Among the blooms, we plant our seeds,
As joy unfolds and gently leads.

The heart beats strong, a rhythmic flow,
The light of day, our hearts bestow.
In every ray, a promise gleams,
Beneath the grasp of golden dreams.

So let us dance in light's embrace,
With every sunrise, find our place.
For in the warmth, our souls unite,
Beneath the sun, forever bright.

Resilient Blooms at First Light

In the garden, dawn unfolds,
Petals glisten, stories told,
Colors bursting, hearts unfold,
Nature's beauty, fierce and bold.

Softly whispers, morning breeze,
Dancing flowers, swaying leaves,
Through the shadows, light retrieves,
Strength in every bloom believes.

Raindrops linger, glistening bright,
Every color, pure delight,
Hopes will rise with day's first light,
Resilient blooms, a wondrous sight.

Rooted deep in earth's embrace,
Growing strong, they find their place,
Chasing warmth, a boundless chase,
Resilient spirit, timeless grace.

In the stillness, silent prayer,
Every flower, a sweet care,
Nature's promise, bold and rare,
Resilient blooms, they always share.

The Scent of Awakening Earth

Beneath the frost, life starts to stir,
Whispers of green, a gentle blur,
Fragrant earth, a soft demur,
Awakening scents, hearts concur.

Decomposed leaves, a rich perfume,
Nature's cycle, born from gloom,
Each new breath dispels the doom,
The scent of life begins to bloom.

Morning dew on blades of grass,
Every raindrop, a spark that lasts,
Whistle of birds, joy unsurpassed,
The awakening, a world recast.

Roots unfurl in soil so deep,
Promises made, secrets to keep,
Awakening earth, dreams to reap,
Nature's rhythm, waking sleep.

As sun climbs high and shadows blend,
All the fragrances gently send,
Hope renewed, with summer's end,
The scent of earth's embrace, our friend.

Rufous Feathers Against the Sky

By the treetops, they take flight,
Rufous feathers, a stunning sight,
Dancing high, a bold delight,
Against the canvas, pure and bright.

With every flap, the world's aglow,
Chasing breezes, soft and slow,
Whispers of freedom as they go,
Rufous dreams in the sunlight's flow.

In harmony with nature's song,
They soar high, where they belong,
Every moment, fierce and strong,
In the sky, they dance along.

Swift and agile, they weave and dive,
In their rhythm, hope will thrive,
Rufous feathers, alive, alive,
With every heartbeat, they survive.

As twilight drapes the sky in hues,
Silent prayers in sunset's blues,
Birds take rest, their path we choose,
Rufous feathers, dusk imbues.

The Clarity of Fresh Beginnings

With morning light, the world awakes,
Each new day, the past forsakes,
Fresh beginnings, the heart remakes,
Clarity shines, as the spirit shakes.

In silence found, the thoughts align,
A blank canvas, a life divine,
Every heartbeat, a bright design,
The clarity, the stars combine.

With every breath, old fears release,
Hope emerges, a sweet increase,
In the stillness, we find peace,
Fresh beginnings never cease.

Rising sun meets morning dew,
In this moment, everything's new,
As the day dawns, dreams pursue,
Clarity flows, like morning's hue.

Together we walk, hand in hand,
Finding strength in the life we've planned,
Fresh beginnings across the land,
The clarity of love, unplanned.

Mornings Wrapped in Light

Golden rays break through the dawn,
Embrace the world, a gentle yawn.
Soft whispers in the waking air,
Each moment cherished, free from care.

The dew-kissed grass, a sparkling sight,
Colors dance with pure delight.
Nature stirs, a vibrant hue,
Morning wraps us in its view.

Birds take flight, their songs arise,
Painting melodies across the skies.
A canvas fresh, the day unfolds,
With every heartbeat, life beholds.

In the warmth of sunlight's glow,
Hope awakens, seeds to sow.
Every heartbeat, a brand new start,
Mornings find us, heart to heart.

Embrace the magic, hold it tight,
In the moment, all feels right.
Let your spirit gently rise,
Mornings wrap us, pure and wise.

Fluttering Wings of Day

Wings unfurl with gentle grace,
Whispers of dawn, a soft embrace.
In the garden, colors sway,
Fluttering wings greet the day.

Nature stirs with every beat,
Life awakens at our feet.
A symphony of sounds combined,
Fluttering wings, our hearts aligned.

Sunlight dances on the leaves,
Joyful hearts, the spirit weaves.
Every flutter, a tale to tell,
In this moment, all is well.

Breezes carry dreams anew,
With each moment, skies turn blue.
Nature's chorus, a gentle sway,
Fluttering wings lead the way.

As the world begins to wake,
New horizons, we shall take.
Fluttering wings, forever stay,
Guiding us through the light of day.

Skylarks Singing Hello

High above, the skylarks soar,
Singing songs forevermore.
Cheerful notes that fill the air,
Welcoming the morning's flare.

Each melody, a joyful sound,
Echoes softly all around.
With every trill, a heart takes flight,
Skylarks greet the dawn with light.

In the meadow, life abounds,
Nature's chorus, joyful sounds.
Skylarks rise and dance so free,
Singing sweetly, 'Come and see.'

Their voices weave a tapestry,
Of warmth and love, a harmony.
A gentle breeze, the day unfolds,
While skylarks share their tales of old.

With each note, our spirits climb,
Skylarks singing, marking time.
In their joy, we find our peace,
As the world awakes, troubles cease.

Hope in Every Glimmer

Stars align in velvet night,
Whispers promise, futures bright.
In the dark, a spark ignites,
Hope in every glimmer lights.

Each flicker tells a tale untold,
Moments cherished, dreams unfold.
To wander where the shadows play,
Finding hope in every ray.

Beneath the sky, our dreams take flight,
Guided by that inner light.
In the hush, as silence grows,
Hope in every glimmer flows.

Through the trials, laughter beams,
Unlocking life's forgotten dreams.
In every tear, and every smile,
Hope in glimmers makes life worthwhile.

As dawn approaches, fears disperse,
Every challenge, we'll immerse.
With open hearts, we'll join the choir,
Hope in every glimmer, our fire.

The Palette of First Light

In soft hues the dawn unfolds,
Brushstrokes of gold and rose,
Whispers of night softly yield,
Nature's canvas, pure and close.

A gentle breeze begins to sway,
Caressing leaves in tender grace,
Colors dance in bright array,
Awakening the silent space.

Birds emerge, their songs so sweet,
Notes that linger, float and play,
A symphony of life, complete,
As daylight banishes the gray.

Shadows retreat, the world ignites,
With every ray a story spun,
The palette glows with fresh delights,
A brand new day has just begun.

Hearts awaken with the sun's first kiss,
Dreams like flowers start to bloom,
In this moment, nothing amiss,
The palette shines, dispelling gloom.

Beneath the Veil of Twilight

As day dips low, the sky's aglow,
With whispers of the coming night,
Stars begin their gentle show,
Embracing all in soft twilight.

The horizon shimmers, fading light,
Casting shadows long and deep,
A world transformed in muted sight,
Where secrets of the dusk do creep.

Cool breezes weave through ancient trees,
Bringing tales from near and far,
They dance with leaves in silent pleas,
Underneath the evening star.

The moon ascends, her face agleam,
A guardian of dreams untold,
In twilight's hush, we find our theme,
As night unfolds its cloak of gold.

Together we stroll, hand in hand,
Lost in the magic of the eve,
With every step, we understand,
Beneath the veil, we learn to believe.

Soft Footsteps on Fresh Dew

Morning breaks with gentle grace,
The earth adorned in silken beads,
A tapestry in nature's space,
Where every drop a story weaves.

Softly tread upon the grass,
Each step a whisper, soft and light,
Dewy gems as moments pass,
Reflecting dawn's awakening bright.

Colors glisten, sparkling clear,
Sunlight kisses the waking world,
The freshness brings a sense so near,
As nature's beauty is unfurled.

Tiny creatures greet the day,
In harmony with vibrant hues,
Life emerges from night's ballet,
As soft footsteps imprint the dews.

With every breath, a treasure found,
In silence, nature's secrets dwell,
On fresh dew, our hopes abound,
In gentle whispers, all is well.

Illuminated Thoughts at Daybreak

With daybreak's light, the mind takes flight,
Ideas bloom like flowers rare,
Illuminated thoughts take sight,
In morning's glow, we pause and stare.

A canvas blank, the heart's delight,
With words that flow like crystal streams,
Each thought a beacon, shining bright,
Guiding us through our waking dreams.

Sunrise paints the world anew,
Chasing shadows, igniting spark,
As clarity pierces through the blue,
Illuminating paths once dark.

In tranquil moments, wisdom stirs,
Inhale the warmth, exhale the night,
With every breath, a thought demurs,
Dancing in the morning light.

As day unfolds, we stand in awe,
Of all the wonders yet to find,
Illuminated by nature's law,
At daybreak, we embrace the mind.

Shadows Retreating

In the hush of fading light,
Figures stretch and blend from view.
Whispers of the night take flight,
As dawn breaks with colors anew.

Silhouettes dance in retreat,
Their secrets hidden, softly spun.
Echoes fade beneath my feet,
As hope awakens with the sun.

The world sheds its darkened skin,
Rebirth as shadows start to wane.
Light cascades, warmth flows within,
Embracing all, invoking change.

Morning stretches, yawns arise,
Birds alight on branches high.
Dreams dissolve, as daylight flies,
Awakening under the sky.

In this glow, new paths appear,
With every heartbeat, life ignites.
I welcome peace, no more fears,
In morning's arms, the future bright.

The Palette of Dawn

Brushstrokes paint the waking morn,
With hues of blush and gentle gold.
A canvas fresh, the day reborn,
Nature's beauty, stories told.

Emerald fields, kissed by dew,
Crimson skies, the sun ascends.
The world unveils its vibrant hue,
As night releases, daylight bends.

Chasing shadows, light ignites,
In every corner, warmth unfolds.
Whispers flit like paper kites,
And dreams emerge, their tales retold.

The clouds stretch wide, a pastel sea,
As flowers bloom, their fragrance sweet.
In this moment, hearts fly free,
The palette shifts beneath our feet.

Through painted skies, my spirit soars,
In dawn's embrace, life feels profound.
With every shade, the heart explores,
The beauty wrapped in light is found.

Beneath the Veil of Twilight

Whispers linger in the air,
As stars begin to twinkle bright.
A shroud of peace, beyond compare,
The world is cloaked in soft twilight.

The horizon melts in shades of blue,
While silhouettes embrace the night.
As day fades gently, dreams come true,
In this serene, enchanting light.

Crickets sing their evening song,
Soft murmurs wrap the earth in grace.
In twilight's arms, we all belong,
In shadows, love finds its place.

The moon awakens with soft sighs,
Casting silver on fields of gold.
In every glance, a spark replies,
Stories of the night unfold.

Beneath the veil where magic breathes,
We dance in time, lost in the glow.
With every heartbeat, the heart believes,
In twilight's charm, we come to know.

Daybreak's Quiet Revelations

In the silence, secrets bloom,
As night surrenders to the dawn.
A chorus hums, dispelling gloom,
In soft light, life's mysteries drawn.

Golden threads weave through the air,
A tapestry that wants to share.
Each ray reveals the paths we tread,
With every heartbeat, hope is fed.

Gentle breezes stir the trees,
As nature stretches, yawns awake.
In this moment, I find my ease,
In daybreak's warmth, my heart shall quake.

Footsteps echo on the ground,
Morning whispers stories sweet.
In quiet revelations found,
Life's rhythm dances, pure and fleet.

With open arms, I greet the light,
Embracing all that lies ahead.
In daybreak's grasp, everything feels right,
As hope and dreams are gently fed.

Murmurs of Forgotten Dreams

In twilight's hush, they softly sigh,
Whispers of hopes that drifted by.
Flickering lights from distant shores,
Awakening souls to dream once more.

Forgotten songs of yesteryear,
Echo through shadows, crystal clear.
A tapestry woven with threads of grace,
Guiding us home to a sacred space.

In quiet corners, memories linger,
Brush of time's soft, tender finger.
Chasing the moon, we find our way,
To the hidden dreams that gently sway.

Lost in the night, our wishes soar,
Each heartbeat calls for something more.
A symphony of silent hopes,
Rising like tides on ocean slopes.

From ashes old, new visions gleam,
A fire ignited, a daring dream.
As dawn breaks softly, shadows flee,
Whispers transform to wild, bold glee.

The Soundtrack of Awakening

Morning light creeps through the blinds,
With soft notes played by nature's finds.
Birds chirp in harmony, bright and clear,
Setting the stage for a brand-new year.

Rustling leaves dance in the breeze,
A chorus of peace that aims to please.
Branches sway, a gentle hum,
Nature's orchestra, just begun.

Awake with dreams still in our sight,
The pulse of the day, a pure delight.
Heartbeats sync with the world outside,
A tune of life, where hopes reside.

Clouds drift like soft, fleeting notes,
Each moment's rhythm lovingly floats.
Sunbeams filter through morning dew,
Painting the skies in shades anew.

In every heartbeat, a story unfolds,
Crafted in whispers, bravely bold.
As we rise to meet the day's embrace,
The soundtrack of life sets the pace.

Sunrise Secrets

Soft hues grace the awakening sky,
As dreams dissolve and shadows lie.
Golden rays touch the sleeping earth,
Revealing magic, a brand-new birth.

Whispers of dawn speak secrets untold,
In tender light, the world unfolds.
Petals unfurl with the sun's sweet breath,
A promise of life beyond the depth.

Birds take flight in joyful arcs,
Tracing their paths through nature's parks.
Rays of warmth kiss the dew-drenched grass,
Time pauses softly, as moments pass.

With each new day, we are reborn,
Carrying hope through the early morn.
In the silence, where dreams reside,
Sunrise secrets cannot hide.

Awakening whispers paint the air,
A gentle nudge to take the dare.
In every dawn, a gift bestowed,
To chase the light on this winding road.

Radiance in Simple Moments

In twilight's glow, we find our peace,
A sweet escape, where worries cease.
Laughter shared over cups of tea,
Moments like these, pure jubilee.

Gentle glances and knowing smiles,
Make the mundane feel worthwhile.
In every heartbeat, joy is found,
In simple things, our love unbound.

The rustling leaves, a soft embrace,
Nature's whisper in this sacred space.
Holding hands as the sun goes down,
Finding light where shadows frown.

In quiet talks under starlit skies,
We weave our dreams, watch time fly.
Radiance glows in the smallest deeds,
Where kindness blooms and love proceeds.

Each heartbeat sings a melody sweet,
In every moment, life feels complete.
Together we find a gentle way,
In simple moments, love will stay.

The Stillness Before the Storm

The winds hold their breath in fright,
The sky turns a deeper hue,
Clouds gather with poised might,
Nature waits, as if it knew.

Birds hush their songs in fear,
Trees bend with a knowing sigh,
The distant rumble draws near,
Stars hide as the day slips by.

Crickets cease their evening song,
Shadows lengthen in the night,
The world pauses, nothing wrong,
In this stillness, there's pure light.

A heartbeat echoes in the air,
Lightning flickers, sharp and bright,
Nature's throne feels its great care,
As silence births the coming fight.

A surge of power starts to rise,
The sky cracks open with a roar,
In the calm, beneath dark skies,
There lies the strength of nature's core.

Tranquil Blues and Oranges

Beneath the twilight's soft embrace,
Blues meld with the orange glow,
A canvas stretched across our space,
A tranquil night begins to flow.

Rippling waters reflect the hues,
Whispers of life in gentle waves,
Where day fades into evening blues,
And starlight with its calmness saves.

Moments linger, soft and sweet,
Where laughter dances with the light,
In this realm, where hearts can meet,
The world slows down, just feels so right.

Holding hands, we find our way,
Through colored skies that never fade,
In tranquil dreams where we can lay,
Our worries washed, the soul unmade.

And when the dawn breaks bright and clear,
The blues blend with the morning fire,
A promise lives beyond the sphere,
In each new day, our hearts conspire.

Sipping Serenity

A cup of warmth held in my hands,
Steam rises, a gentle embrace,
Time slows down, in dreamlike lands,
A moment found, a sacred space.

Each sip unravels the day's weight,
Revealing thoughts, both deep and light,
A quiet ritual, my true fate,
In sips of peace, I find my sight.

Sunrise spills through the window pane,
Golden rays dance on the floor,
The world awakens, free of pain,
As I savor, I crave for more.

In every drop, a story flows,
A blend of spices, warmth, and spice,
With every taste, serenity grows,
In this moment, all feels so nice.

So here I sit, in blissful cheer,
With hopes that linger in the air,
Sipping slowly, holding what's near,
In a world that shows it truly cares.

Ethereal Light

Morning's whisper breaks the night,
Softly draping the world in grace,
An ethereal glow, pure and bright,
In every corner, in every space.

Golden beams pierce the morning haze,
And dance upon the tender dew,
Wrapped in warmth, the sun's embrace,
Brings life anew, a canvas true.

Waves of color stretch across the field,
Gentle breezes woven tight,
Secrets that nature has revealed,
In the glow, our souls take flight.

Birds take wing, gliding so free,
Harmonies blend in the sky's delight,
As day breaks forth, wild and carefree,
Captured in this ethereal light.

With every moment, magic swells,
Illuminating all that we see,
In tranquil whispers, the heart compels,
To thrive where love and light will be.

Echoes of a New Day

Whispers of dawn fill the air,
As shadows retreat from their lair.
Birds sing sweet songs up high,
While the sun begins to rise.

Nature stirs with vibrant grace,
All life joins in this embrace.
Colors burst, a brilliant show,
In the light's warm golden glow.

Hopes awaken with the light,
Casting off the cloak of night.
Moments precious, swiftly go,
Tales of time we come to know.

The world turns with gentle cheer,
As dreams of yesterday disappear.
Each breath a promise we make,
A journey new, for hope's sake.

In echoes of a brand new day,
We find our hearts along the way.
With every sunrise, we reframe,
The story of our lives, aflame.

The Sun's Gentle Embrace

The sun peeks over the hill,
A soft warmth that soothes and thrills.
With each ray, the shadows flee,
In its glow, we feel so free.

Nature stirs in a sweet ballet,
With whispers of a brand new day.
Petals open, dew drops gleam,
In the sunlight's tender dream.

Birds take flight, a symphony,
In unison, they sing for me.
Their melodies dance through the air,
As I pause and breathe, aware.

The world wrapped in golden light,
Every moment feels just right.
The sun's embrace, a warm caress,
Filling hearts with happiness.

In this haven, time slows down,
Peace envelops all around.
As day unfolds, I find my place,
In the sun's gentle embrace.

A Symphony of Awakening

Morning breaks, a sweet refrain,
Nature's orchestra starts again.
The stretching sun brings forth its tune,
A melody beneath the moon.

Rustling leaves and chirping prize,
As daylight spills across the skies.
Each note a promise, fresh and clear,
Whispered softly in your ear.

From hills and valleys, voices rise,
In harmony, beneath the skies.
A symphony composed with care,
In every breath, a song to share.

The world awakens from its sleep,
As memories of dreams we keep.
Together, hearts begin to sway,
In this dance of the new day.

With every beat, we find our way,
Guided by the sun's ballet.
In this symphony we play,
Awakening, come what may.

Mornings Untold

Every morning, a blank slate,
With mysteries we contemplate.
A canvas stretched beyond our view,
Awaits the strokes of me and you.

Gold and pink paint the sky,
As sleepy clouds drift slowly by.
With each hue, a story spins,
Of all the journeys that begin.

Footsteps echo on the street,
As dawn's light makes the world complete.
Each day a treasure, bright and bold,
In the tales of mornings untold.

With coffee brewing, laughter flows,
In shared moments, our love grows.
Hope arises with the sun,
In every heart, a race begun.

For each sunrise brings a chance,
To dream anew, to take a stance.
In mornings untold, we embrace,
The beauty of time and space.

Gatherings of Ghostly Shadows

In the twilight where whispers play,
Shadows gather at the end of day.
Memories dance in the fading light,
Ghostly visions in the still of night.

Echoes linger in the softest breeze,
Tales of yore that bring me to my knees.
Figures shimmer in the moon's soft glow,
As I wander where the lost ones go.

A cool chill wraps around my spine,
Phantoms gather, entwined in line.
Secrets shared in a silent space,
In their presence, I find solace's grace.

Unseen voices call from afar,
Guiding me beneath the evening star.
Through the mist, they beckon me near,
In ghostly gatherings, I feel no fear.

As the night deepens, shadows twine,
A spectral dance, old tales combine.
In their arms, I find the thread,
Of all the lives that once were led.

Breathing in Possibilities

Each dawn unfolds like a new dream,
Awakening hope with its gentle beam.
I breathe in deeply, the morning starts,
Filling my soul with joyous arts.

The world awakens, colors ignite,
Every moment feels warm and bright.
Possibilities swirl in the air,
An uncharted path, I'm tempted to dare.

Nature sings in a vibrant tune,
As possibilities bloom like flowers in June.
With each step taken, the heart does race,
Exploring paths in a wide-open space.

Worries fade in the fresh morning light,
Every breath brings a world of delight.
Expanding dreams on the wings of the day,
I'll gather my courage and find my way.

With an open heart, I journey far,
Chasing the glow of my own North Star.
Breathing in life, oh what a thrill,
I am alive, and I always will.

Exploring Morning's Embrace

Morning whispers secrets soft and low,
Inviting me where bright rivers flow.
Sunrise paints the sky in hues so bold,
A canvas unfurling, a story told.

With each ray, a promise to behold,
Life awakens in shades of gold.
I wander through dew-kissed fields serene,
In the heart of morning, all is pristine.

Birds take flight on wings of grace,
Nature's canvas, a tranquil space.
Each leaf dances, caught in the breeze,
Embracing moments, discovering ease.

The scent of blooms fills the vibrant air,
In morning's embrace, I find my share.
The world unfolds, a treasure to find,
In the gentle embrace, I leave worries behind.

As dawn unfolds, I savor the day,
In morning's arms, I shall not stray.
With hope ignited, I journey anew,
In exploring the morning, I'm reborn too.

Fields of Gold

Winds weave through the fields so wide,
Where golden grains like oceans glide.
Sunlight dances on blush and bloom,
Nature's whispers dispel all gloom.

Every stalk sways with a gentle grace,
In this haven, I find my space.
Colors blend in a soft embrace,
Fields of gold, my secret place.

Beneath the sky, endless and blue,
I lose myself in the beauty true.
Birds take flight, singing sweet tunes,
In this sanctuary beneath the moons.

As shadows stretch with the setting sun,
The day unfolds, its course well-run.
I breathe in deeply and feel so whole,
In the fields of gold, I unearth my soul.

Every sunset wraps me in its glow,
Transforming the world in a fiery show.
In nature's cradle, peace I unfold,
Forever cherished in these fields of gold.

Golden Haze on the Horizon

In the morning's glow, dreams take flight,
Whispers of dawn, hearts feel light.
Amber rays spill, warm and bold,
A tapestry woven, a story told.

Mountains bathe in a gilded sheen,
Nature wakes, serene and keen.
The sky blushes, a canvas divine,
Golden hues dance, a moment in time.

Waves of light crest the gentle seas,
Swaying softly in a tender breeze.
Promises linger in the day's embrace,
Hope is reborn in this sacred space.

Fields awaken with colors ablaze,
Each petal gleams in the morning's gaze.
A symphony plays, vibrant and clear,
With every heartbeat, the world draws near.

Hands reaching out to touch the glow,
In this golden haze, we find our flow.
Breath of life, in the warmth we bask,
As the horizon whispers, we dare to ask.

Traces of Night's Farewell

Veils of twilight start to fade,
Stars retreat, their light delayed.
Moonlight slips beneath the sea,
Whispers of night, setting free.

Shadows soften, surrendering slow,
A gentle sigh, the dawn's first show.
Winds carry secrets, tender and light,
Kissing the remnants of the night.

Clouds blush softly as dawn appears,
Echoes of dreams, fading fears.
Glistening dew on the blades of grass,
Nature's diary, moments that pass.

Birds break silence, their songs awake,
A melody sweet, a new day to make.
The world stretches, yawns with delight,
Traces of night lost in the light.

As night concedes to the sun's embrace,
Life gathers warmth, finds its pace.
In the aftermath, hope takes its stand,
With traces of night cradled in hand.

Rituals of Awakening

Delicate whispers of dawn unfold,
Promises kept, stories retold.
Morning breathes with tender grace,
In the stillness, time finds its place.

Nature stirs in a symphonic rise,
Sunlight dances in joyous skies.
Every leaf with a shimmer bright,
Welcomes the day, bids farewell to night.

Rituals echo in the cool of air,
An ancient song, a timeless prayer.
Awakening hearts in rhythm and rhyme,
Cherishing moments, holding onto time.

With every heartbeat, the world ignites,
Awakening souls to mesmerizing sights.
As shadows retreat, dreams intertwine,
In rituals rich, our spirits shine.

Awake, alive, with hope in our chest,
To dance with the dawn, to live and to rest.
In this sacred space, let the magic unfold,
As rituals of life we lovingly hold.

Dawn's Soft Caress

In the quiet hour where dreams converge,
Dawn stretches slowly, a gentle surge.
Soft light spills over the waking earth,
Bringing with it the promise of birth.

Colors blend in a tender embrace,
Kissing the hills with a warm grace.
The air, sweet with the scent of dew,
Heralds the day, bursting anew.

Gentle breezes play in the trees,
Carrying whispers of soulful pleas.
Each note a reminder, a soothing song,
In dawn's soft caress, we all belong.

Time stretches out in a golden haze,
The world awakens to life's grand praise.
Moments collected, cherished and rare,
Wrapped in the warmth of morning's snare.

As sunlight spills on the waking land,
Nature rejoices, hand in hand.
In the magic of dawn, hearts take flight,
Finding solace in the embrace of light.

Renewal in Every Breath

In the dawn of morning light,
Hope awakens, taking flight.
Nature sighs in peaceful grace,
Life resumes its gentle pace.

With each breath, a new beginning,
Softly fades the night's cold spinning.
Awakened hearts, newly sewn,
In the stillness, love is grown.

The world hums a quiet tune,
Melodies beneath the moon.
Every heartbeat, whispers deep,
Promises that life will keep.

Brush the past with gentle ease,
Find solace in blooming trees.
Every moment holds a chance,
To embrace the sacred dance.

Renewed faith begins to spark,
Lighting shadows in the dark.
With every breath, faith will rise,
In the dawn, our spirits fly.

Whispers of the Breeze

In the garden, secrets sway,
Carried softly on the day.
Leaves converse in rustling tones,
Nature's speech, a world of loans.

Breezes tease the fragile flowers,
Dancing through the brightened hours.
Every petal, every grain,
Carries whispers, soft like rain.

The air is filled with tales untold,
Of dreams pursued, and hearts so bold.
Gentle breezes breathe anew,
Speaking softly, just to you.

Through the trees, a laughter sings,
Carried on the wind's soft wings.
Nature's comfort, sweet and clear,
Reminds us that our home is near.

Whispers dance on summer nights,
Easing souls with gentle lights.
In the stillness, joy transcends,
In the breeze, our hearts make amends.

Anticipation in the Air

Clouds gather, stories rise,
Artistry of painted skies.
Fields await the falling rain,
Nourished roots, beginning strain.

A hush settles, time draws near,
Every heartbeat feels the fear.
Promise of the wild unknown,
In the garden's heart, it's sown.

Scent of freshness in the breeze,
Whispers echo through the trees.
Every moment holds a spark,
In the night, anticipating dark.

Hope weaves through the cosmic thread,
As dreams dance through what's said.
In the silence, belly deep,
Restless hearts that yearn and leap.

Count the beats, a worldly tune,
Feeling life beneath the moon.
Anticipation paints the sky,
In each heartbeat, dreams will fly.

Clocks Ticking to Dawn's Rhythm

The clocks tick soft, a gentle call,
Marking moments, great and small.
Each second whispers time's embrace,
Carving paths we dare to trace.

As shadows dance with fading light,
Waking dreams from endless night.
In the ticks, a cadence flows,
Guiding hearts where wisdom grows.

Hands of time move slow and sure,
Each beat echoes, hearts endure.
In the rhythm, hope takes flight,
Cradled close within the night.

Dawn approaches, soft and bright,
Unlocks treasures, pure delight.
In the waking, life will bloom,
Promises escape the gloom.

The clock ticks on, we feel its grace,
Each heartbeat in this sacred space.
To dawn's rhythm, we belong,
In the silence, sing our song.